CONTENTS

Words in **bold** are explained in the glossary.

What is a tiger?

A tiger is a big, wild cat.

It can weigh more than 250 kilograms.
An adult tiger may be up to three metres
long with a metre-long tail.

Tiger

World map

Asia

4   Tigers live in Asia. Some live in hot jungles
and **swamps**. Others live in cold forests.

Lions, leopards and cheetahs are also big cats.

Lion

Leopard

Cheetah

Tigers are the biggest members of the cat family.

What does a tiger look like?

Most tigers have orange fur with black stripes.

The black stripes are good **camouflage** in long grass.

Every tiger has a different pattern of stripes.

Some tigers are white with black stripes and blue eyes.

A tiger has 30 teeth including large **canine teeth** at the front.

It has sharp claws which can be ten centimetres long.

Canine teeth

Meet a tiger cub

This is a tiger cub with his mother.

There are two cubs in the **litter**. They are brothers.

A female tiger normally has two to three cubs at one time.

When they are born tiger cubs are **blind**.

Tiger cub

The cubs and their mother do not live with the cubs' father or any other tigers.

Female tiger

Tiger eyes and markings

The tiger cub will open his eyes when he is about two weeks old.

At first, his eyes will be blue. They will change to yellow when he is older.

All tigers have a special marking called a 'wang mark' on their forehead.

The mark looks like the 'wang' symbol which means 'king' in Chinese.

Looking after the cubs

The mother tiger looks after her cubs very well.

She keeps the cubs safe in a **den** made in a cave or hollow tree.

She washes the cubs by licking them with her rough tongue.

12

If the cubs are in danger from other animals the mother moves them.

She picks them up by the scruff of the neck and carries them in her mouth.

What do tiger cubs eat?

At first the tiger cub and his brother drink only their mother's milk.

When they are about six months old they begin to eat meat caught by their mother.

Tigers hunt animals such as deer, wild pigs, monkeys and birds.

Learning to hunt

Tiger cubs learn to hunt by watching their mother. She takes her cubs hunting and they watch her as she sneaks up and jumps on her **prey**.

Then the cubs practise hunting.

They sneak up and jump on each other.

Then they sneak up and jump on
small animals.

When does the tiger cub live on his own?

When the tiger cub is about two or three years old he leaves his mother.

From now on he will live on his own. He will hunt on his own, too, usually at night.

He marks his **territory** in the forest by scratching the trees and roaring if other tigers come close.

A tiger's roar can be heard from three kilometres away.

Tigers in danger

Many tigers are hunted and killed for their fur.

The forests and jungles where tigers live are being cut down to make space for farms and houses.

If the forests and jungles are cut down, the tigers will have nowhere to live.

There are only about 8,000 tigers left in the world.

Glossary

blind

Not able to see.

camouflage

Skin markings or fur colour that make an animal hard to see.

canine teeth

Long, pointed teeth at the front of the mouth which are used for biting and tearing food.

den

The home of a
wild animal.

litter

A group of animals
born at the same time.

prey

An animal that is
hunted by another
animal for food.

swamps

Very wet places with
lots of pools, streams
and water plants.

territory

The area where an animal lives
and where it finds its food.

23

Index

Copyright © ticktock Entertainment Ltd 2008
First published in Great Britain in 2008 by ticktock Media Ltd.
Unit 2, Orchard Business Centre, North Farm Road, Tunbridge Wells, Kent TN2 3XF
ISBN 978 1 84696 770 2 pbk
Printed in China

We would like to thank: Penny Worms, Shirley Bickler, Suzanne Baker and the National Literacy Trust.

Picture credits (t=top, b=bottom, c=centre, l-left, r=right, OFC= outside front cover)
Alamy: 13, 24. Corbis: 4, 5, 16, 19, 20, 21. FLPA: 1, 10. Getty: 14. Photolibrary (Oxford Scientific): 12, 15. Superstock: 6, 7, 8-9, 11, 17, 18.

Every effort has been made to trace the copyright holders, and we apologise in advance for any unintentional omissions. We would be pleased to insert the appropriate acknowledgements in any subsequent edition of this publication.